Circular Knitting Machine Patterns

Basic Circular Knitting Machine Patterns For Beginners

Copyright © 2023

All rights reserved.

DEDICATION

The author and publisher have provided this e-book to you for your personal use only. You may not make this e-book publicly available in any way. Copyright infringement is against the law. If you believe the copy of this e-book you are reading infringes on the author's copyright, please notify the publisher at: https://us.macmillan.com/piracy

Circular Knitting Machine Patterns

Contents

Giant Pool Noodle Rainbow Wall Hanging 1

Addi Boho Towel Ring 6

Maci Beanie 16

Colorful Twist Headband 22

Addi Bear Lovey 27

Machine Knit Bags for Christmas 48

Simple 4-Minute Bow 55

Circular Knitting Machine Patterns

Giant Pool Noodle Rainbow Wall Hanging

SUPPLIES NEEDED

5 pool noodles

Sharp Scissors

22 Pin Knitting Machine

Circular Knitting Machine Patterns

Worsted Weight Yarn

Varsity Red

Orange

Varsity Gold

Light Green

Varsity Blue

Grape

Super Bulky Weight Yarn

Lettuce Knife or Utility Knife for cutting pool noodles, though sharp scissors work fine too

Long Plastic Yarn Needle

Circular Knitting Machine Patterns

Measure and cut each of the pool noodles

Red – 48", this will be covered with a red knit tube.

Red – 41", this will be covered with an orange knit tube.

Green – 33", this will be covered with a yellow knit tube.

Green – 26.25", this will be covered with a green knit tube.

Blue – 21", this will be covered with a blue knit tube.

Circular Knitting Machine Patterns

Red – 7", this should be leftover from the other red tube and will be covered with 2 purple knit tubes.

Time to get out the knitting machine and crank out the following rows in each color.

Orange – 193 rows

Yellow – 160 rows

Green – 123 rows

Blue – 93 rows

Purple – 40 rows (make 2)

Once all of the tubes have been knitted, slide them over each of the tubes. Now you are ready to put the wall hanging together.

Circular Knitting Machine Patterns

Addi Boho Towel Ring

Supplies Needed:

-Addi 22 pin circular knitting machine

-26-30 yds of worsted weight yarn in main color

Circular Knitting Machine Patterns

-5 yds of waste yarn

-Size G 4.25 mm hook

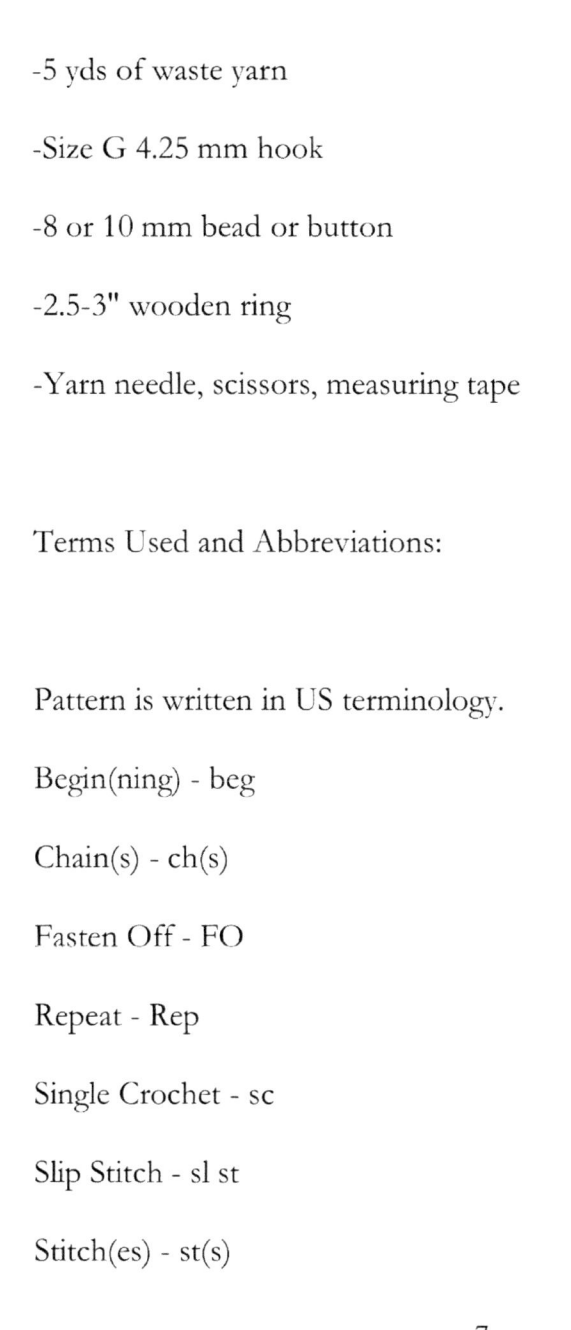

-8 or 10 mm bead or button

-2.5-3" wooden ring

-Yarn needle, scissors, measuring tape

Terms Used and Abbreviations:

Pattern is written in US terminology.

Begin(ning) - beg

Chain(s) - ch(s)

Fasten Off - FO

Repeat - Rep

Single Crochet - sc

Slip Stitch - sl st

Stitch(es) - st(s)

Circular Knitting Machine Patterns

Yarn Over - YO

Gauge:

8 sts and 10 rows = 2" (5 cm) using medium tension for knitted portion. Gauge for crocheted portion is not imperative.

Finished Measurements:

Tube was stretched and then allowed to relax before laying flat and taking the measurements. Unfinished tube measures approx. 7.5" (19 cm) prior to assembly and not including waste yarn.

Pattern Notes:

-All cast-on and cast-off methods used in this pattern will be the provisional (basic) cast-on and cast-off methods.

Circular Knitting Machine Patterns

-You will need to be able to read and follow basic beginner crochet pattern instructions.

-You will need to understand basic sewing techniques.

Instructions:

Towel ring is made by cinching one end of knitted tube and closing other end with sl st method. It is then crocheted to the wooden ring using basic crochet sts. A wooden bead is added for a button and the tassel (optional) is added last.

Towel Tube

1) Cast on with main color and knit 35 rows.

2) Leaving yourself a long tail for sewing and crocheting purposes later, cut yarn and add waste yarn. Knit 5 more rows.

3) Cast off.

Assembly

1) Beg with cast-on end and cinch shut. Thread yarn needle onto tail and reinforce your sts by taking the tail through all sts once more. Knot off but do not cut yarn.

Insert crochet hook into cast-on bottom near center and pull up a loop with leftover tail. Ch 5 (ch more if your button is larger), sl st into cast-on bottom once more to create a ch loop. This loop will be our button hole. FO and weave tail into tube.

Circular Knitting Machine Patterns

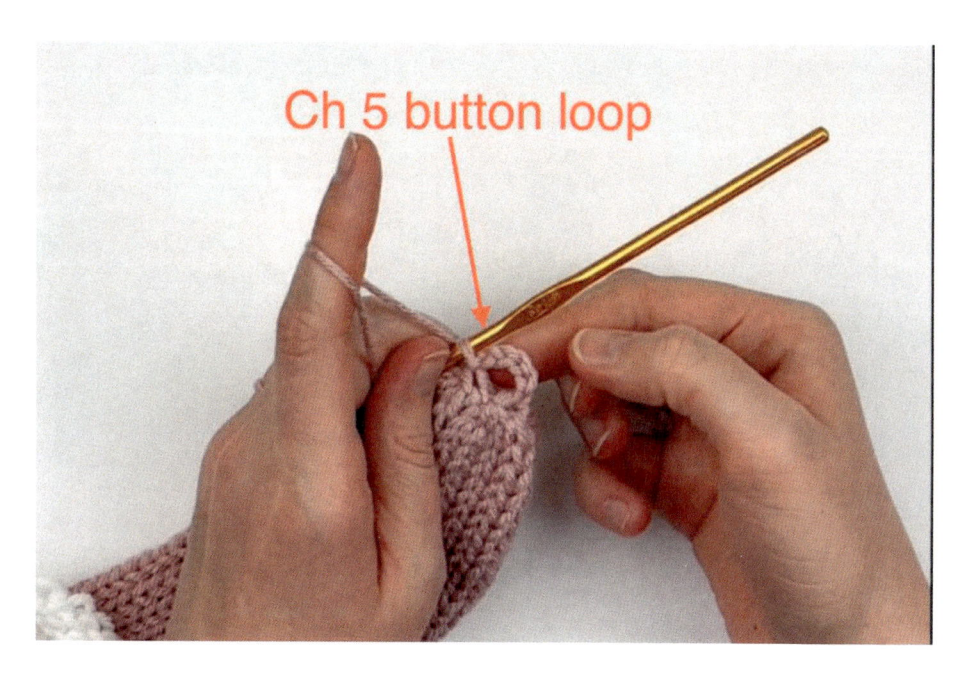

Ch 5 button loop

1) Line sts up at cast-off end and use the sl st method to close. (Remember to leave your tail long for the next portion.) Remove waste yarn.

Insert your hook into the sl st nearest your long tail. Grab your wooden ring and attach it following these steps below.

a. Place wooden ring between your working yarn (long tail) and your hook. Going through the wooden ring, make a sl st.

Circular Knitting Machine Patterns

Place ring between working yarn & hook. Draw yarn through ring and sl st

b.   Move wooden ring to the right of your work and insert your hook into 1st sl st once more. Pull up a loop (you should have 2 loops on your hook).

c.   Move ring back between your hook and working yarn. Going through the ring, YO and draw through both loops on your hook.

Circular Knitting Machine Patterns

Move ring between hook & working yarn. Go through ring and draw yarn through both loops

d. Rep steps A-C in every other sl st across until you reach the end. You should have a total of 11 sc when you are done.

Repeat process in every other st to end

e. Sl st into piece once more and FO, weaving in your tail.

Add your bead

With a small length of yarn and your yarn needle, sew your bead onto the front of the towel ring, about mid-way down. If you are adding a tassel, be sure to leave a bit of space below the bead for the tassel to hang. Take tails to inside of tube.

Add your tassel

1) Wrap your fingers/cardboard 7 times and cut bottoms to create tassel tails.

2) Take one end of all 7 tails through your button hole and bring ends together to make them even (It doesn't have to be perfect. We will cut the tails later).

3) Using the Gathering Knot, secure the tassel tails just below the button hole/loop. Cut off the excess and trim the tassel tails to be even.

Circular Knitting Machine Patterns

Maci Beanie

Supplies Needed:

Addi Express King Size Knitting Machine

Circular Knitting Machine Patterns

Yarn: 2 colors of Worsted Weight Yarn (1/2 ball each or 1 ball for a solid hat)

Suggested Yarn: We Are Knitters, The Petite Wool

Yardage: 76 yards of each color or 153 yards of one color.

Waste Yarn: Waste yarn in a contrasting color to your hat.

Notions: Red Needle that comes with your Addi Machine (or bent darning needle), Pick/Hook that comes with your Addi or a bent paperclip. scissors, faux fur pom (Optional).

Gauge:

12sts x 22rounds

Circular Knitting Machine Patterns

Finished Measurements:

8" wide x 11" tall

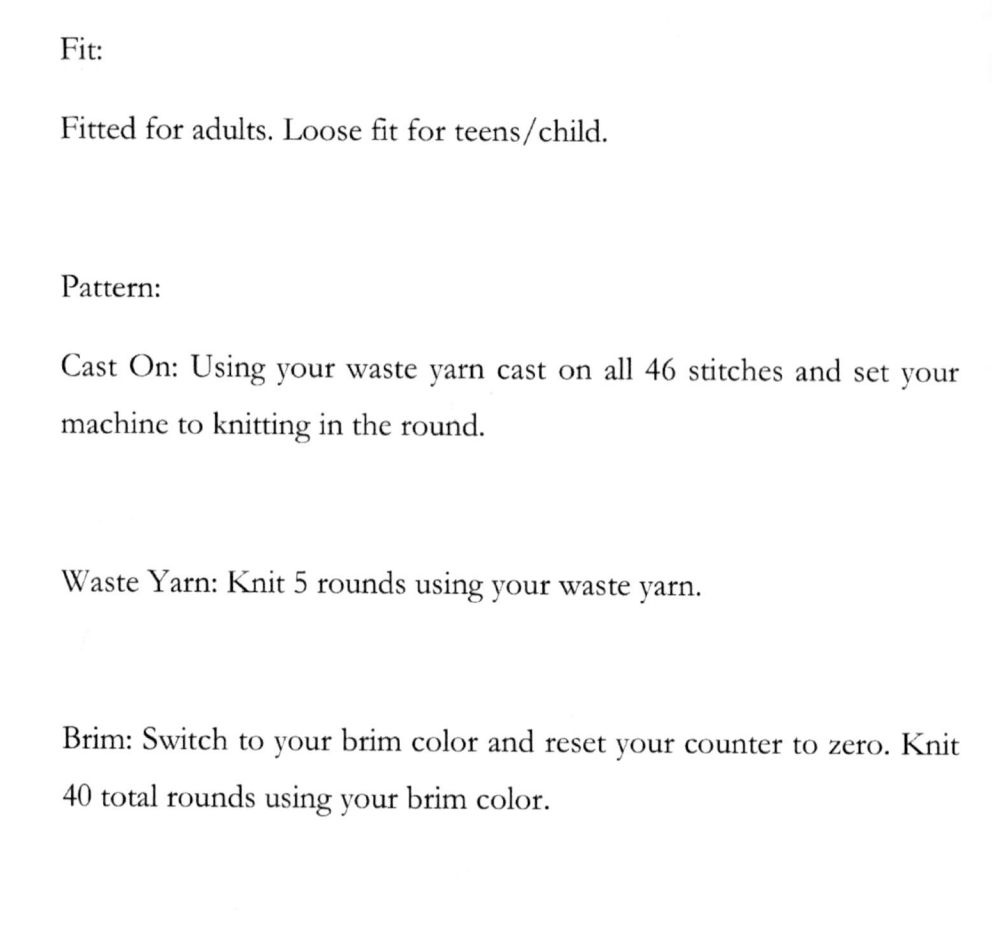

Fit:

Fitted for adults. Loose fit for teens/child.

Pattern:

Cast On: Using your waste yarn cast on all 46 stitches and set your machine to knitting in the round.

Waste Yarn: Knit 5 rounds using your waste yarn.

Brim: Switch to your brim color and reset your counter to zero. Knit 40 total rounds using your brim color.

Circular Knitting Machine Patterns

Create Double Brim: Using your hook/pick, starting with the first brim color loop to the left of the tail next to the waste yarn. Pick up each loop and place it up on the needle. Slowly turn the handle keeping light tension on the working yarn so not to drop any stitches. Work around picking up every first stitch of the brim color and bringing it up to the needle.

Continue Brim: Still using the brim color, knit 5 more rounds.

Top Color: Switch to the top color and knit until your counter reads 70 TOTAL rounds.

Circular Knitting Machine Patterns

Cut Waste Yarn: Cut your waste yarn off in sections and remove it from the brim. Making sure to cut only the waste yarn and not your brim color.

Circular Knitting Machine Patterns

Cast Off: Cast off all stitches while they are still on the machine. To do so, cut your working yarn approximately 2 feet long. Thread your working yarn onto the red needle that came with your Addi or a bent darning needle. Turning your machine slowly, place your needle under each stitch as you come to them and thread the needle through each stitch. Thread the yarn through all of the stitches and pull tight to close. Sew the remaining yarn through the top of your hat a few times to close.

Finishing: Weave in ends, block and attach a pom if you like!

Circular Knitting Machine Patterns

Colorful Twist Headband

Supplies Needed:

Addi Express King Size Knitting Machine

Circular Knitting Machine Patterns

Yarn: 2 colors of Fingering Weight Yarn (1/3 ball (133 yards) each or 1 ball (133 yards) of worsted weight yarn for a solid headband)

Suggested Yarn: Knit Picks – Hawthorne Speckle Handpainted, Knit Picks – Muse Hand Painted Sock Yarn, Knit Picks – Stroll Hand Painted. (Or some of your favorite indie dyed yarn)

Yardage: 76 yards of each color or 153 yards of one color.

Waste Yarn: Waste yarn in a contrasting color.

Notions: Scissors, 4.00mm Crochet Hook, Tapestry Needle.

Gauge:

12sts x 22rounds

Finished Measurements:

8" wide x 6" tall – after seaming

Fit:

Fitted for adults. Loose fit for teens/child.

Circular Knitting Machine Patterns

Pattern:

Cast On: Using your waste yarn cast on all 46 stitches and set your machine to knitting in the round.

Waste Yarn: Knit 5-7 rounds using your waste yarn.

Headband: Switch to your headband colors. Leaving a 2 foot tail for seaming and holding both strands of fingering weight yarns at the same time begin knitting with your main colors. Remember to reset your counter to zero. Knit 77 total rounds using your headband colors.

Waste Yarn: Break your main color yarns leaving a 10" tail and put your waste yarn back onto your machine. Knit 5-7 rounds using your waste yarn.

Cast Off: Cast off all stitches by simply turning your machine and letting the stitches fall off the needles.

Circular Knitting Machine Patterns

Closing Up the Ends: Close each end using your crochet hook and starting at the side opposite your tail. Place your crochet hook through the first stitch of the main color and the stitch that's furthest away from the tail. Pull the first stitch to the right of that loop through the first loop. Go across to the left side and grab that first stitch and pull it through the current stitch on your hook. To see this in detail please see min 11:50 of the video tutorial. Continue down the side grabbing the next stitch/loop and pulling it through the current stitch on your hook. Once you have reached the end where your tail is pull the tail through your final stitch to secure and close it up.

Now pull off the waste yarn for that side by unraveling it or cutting it and pulling it out. Being careful not to cut the main headband.

Repeat this closure for the other end of the headband.

Seaming: Lay your headband flat on the table. Take one end and turn it over 180 degrees to create a twist in the middle of the headband.

Now bring both ends together in the middle. Seam these ends together using the mattress stitch. See min 20:00 in the video tutorial for additional details.

Finishing: Weave ends in between both sides of the headband through the seam to secure.

Circular Knitting Machine Patterns

Addi Bear Lovey

MATERIALS

– Worsted weight yarn. Im using Yarn Bee Soft and Sleek from Hobby Lobby in the color Brownie.

– Scrap yarn for the snout, nose and eyes of your Addi Bear.

– Addi Express Kingsize knitting machine

Circular Knitting Machine Patterns

– H Crochet Hook

– Polyfil

– 2 Stitch Markers

– Tapestry Needle

– Scissors

– Logo Tag (optional)

– 22mm Noise Maker Insert (optional)

Circular Knitting Machine Patterns

PATTERN

INNER HEAD

No waste yarn for this part.

Cast on your yarn, crank out 16 rows, then cast off by using a tapestry needle and picking up each stitch at a time to take it off the machine.

Circular Knitting Machine Patterns

Pull closed your first tail then use your tapestry needle to completely close and secure it.

Start to gently pull your second tail, slowly closing the top hole.

Stuff with polyfill and your noisemaker and continue closing the rest of the way. Use a tapestry needle again to fully close and secure the second hole.

Tie off and hide your tails inside of your head.

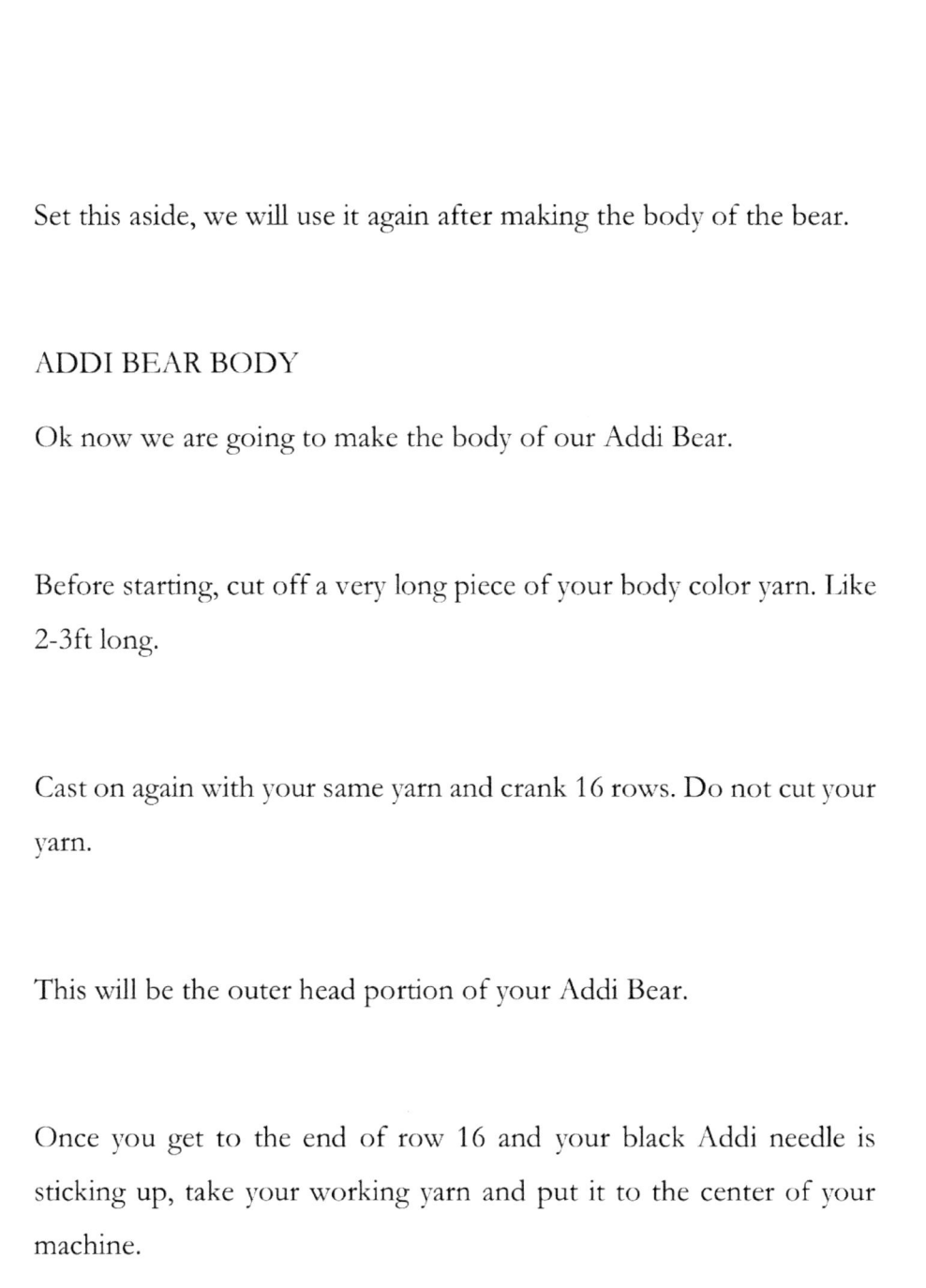

Set this aside, we will use it again after making the body of the bear.

ADDI BEAR BODY

Ok now we are going to make the body of our Addi Bear.

Before starting, cut off a very long piece of your body color yarn. Like 2-3ft long.

Cast on again with your same yarn and crank 16 rows. Do not cut your yarn.

This will be the outer head portion of your Addi Bear.

Once you get to the end of row 16 and your black Addi needle is sticking up, take your working yarn and put it to the center of your machine.

Circular Knitting Machine Patterns

Grab your "pull yarn" and do one full row using the "pull yarn" instead of your working yarn. Kinda like making a stripe with your "pull yarn".

Switch back to your main working yarn, leaving the tails of your "pull yarn" do dangle in the center of your work.

Crank out 43 more rows of the body of your bear.

End by cranking a few rows of waste yarn in a contrasting color then cast off.

SEEMING UP THE BOTTOM OF YOUR BEAR BODY

Place a stitch marker in the very last loop made before you switched to your waste yarn.

Go ahead and make sure your body color tail isn't tucked into your work and is hanging on the outside. You will need this here in a bit.

Starting from your first loop before your waste yarn row, count over 23 stitches. Place another stitch marker there.

This will be the front half of our bear body.

Insert your crochet hook into the loop with the 2nd stitch marker, grab the loop directly next to it, and pull through.

Circular Knitting Machine Patterns

Insert your hook into the next stitch beside the stitch marker (this is on the front side of your bear body now) and pull through.

Continue pulling through loops, alternating between the back half and front half, until you are all the way across the bottom of your bear.

The place where you put your first stitch marker will be your very last stitch.

Secure your work by pulling your tail through the last loop on your hook.

Circular Knitting Machine Patterns

Now you can remove your waste yarn.

Now its time to create the neck of your Addi Bear.

Grab your "pull yarn" tails and gently pull them tight.

Circular Knitting Machine Patterns

Insert your "inner head" then clinch the second head hole by gently pulling the tail.

Close the hole with your tapestry needle, tie off and hide your tail inside the head.

Hid the tail at the bottom of your Addi bear into the body between the front and back panels.

ARMS– MAKE 2

Circular Knitting Machine Patterns

Using your H crochet hook and your body color yarn.

Create a magic circle and CH 1.

Round 1: SC 6 into the center of your magic circle. Pull the circle closed.

Pro Tip: Use a stitch marker here if you need to

Round 2: SC INC in each stitch around (12)

Circular Knitting Machine Patterns

Rounds 3: SC in each stitch around (12)

Sew in your first tail, securing your magic circle.

Rounds 4-15: SC in each stitch around (12)

Cut yarn leaving a long tail for attaching your arm to your Addi Bear.

EARS- MAKE 2

Circular Knitting Machine Patterns

Using your H crochet hook and your body color yarn.

Create a magic circle and CH 1.

Round 1: SC 7 into the center of your magic circle. Pull the circle closed.

Round 2: SC INC in each stitch around (14)

Rounds 3-4: SC in each stitch around (14)

Circular Knitting Machine Patterns

Sew in your tail and secure your magic circle.

Round 5: SC DEC over the first 2 stitches. SC in the next 3 stitches. SC DEC over the next two stitches. SC in the next 3 stitches. SC DEC over the next two stitches. SC in the last 2 stitches (11)

Cut yarn leaving a long tail for attaching your ear to your Addi Bear.

SNOUT

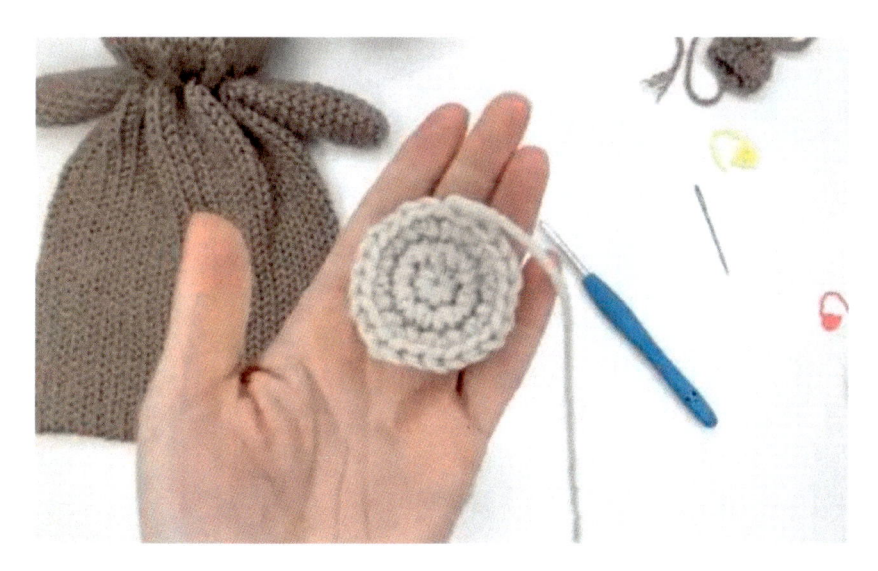

Circular Knitting Machine Patterns

Using your H Hook and Snout color yarn

Create a magic circle and CH 1.

Row 1: SC 8 into your magic circle. Join into the top of your first SC. CH 1.

Row 2: SC INC in each stitch around (16) Join into the top of your first SC. CH 1.

Row 3: *SC in the first stitch, SC INC in the next * Repeat that around for a total of 7 times. (24) Join into the top of your first SC.

Tie off leaving a long tail for sewing your snout onto your Addi Bear. Sew in your first tail.

ADDI BEAR ASSEMBLY

Circular Knitting Machine Patterns

After the arms, we attach the snout.

Using sewing pins, line your snout up on your bear face where you want it to go. Remove the pins as you go.

Using the whip stitch and your tapestry needle so on your snout.

Circular Knitting Machine Patterns

Tie off and hid your tail inside the head of your body.

Now lets embroider the nose.

Grabbing your scrap nose color yarn and a tapestry needle.

Insert your needle in the head of your bear and pop it out where you want the bottom tip of your nose to go.

Insert your needle into the top right corner of your Addi Bear nose and pop out where you want the top left corner to be.

Continue going into the tip of your bear nose and popping out where you want the next strand to lay until your entire nose is created.

Tie off and hide your tail inside your bear head.

EYES AND MOUTH

Embroider the eyes and the mouth using the same method as the nose.

Tie off and hide your tails inside your bear head.

EARS

Using your pins again, begin placing your ears onto your bear head where you think they need to go.

Make any necessary adjustments until you are happy with the placement of your ears, then sew them on with your tapestry needle.

Tie off and hide your tails into the head of your Addi Bear.

TAG- OPTIONAL

Last but not least, sew on your logo tag if you would like.

Circular Knitting Machine Patterns

Machine Knit Bags for Christmas

Materials for Completion:

40 Pin and 46/48 Pin Knitting Machine

Worsted Weight Yarn:

Suggested yarns

Circular Knitting Machine Patterns

Yarn for lining bag – Lion Brand Pound of Love

Yarn for outside of bag – Lion Brand Fisherman's Wool

US Size 7 Circular Knitting Needle used for casting off machine, though other methods of casting off will work

Ribbon

Darning Needle

Scissors

Tension: Tight (first hole only)

Other supplies:

Row Counter

Circular Knitting Machine Patterns

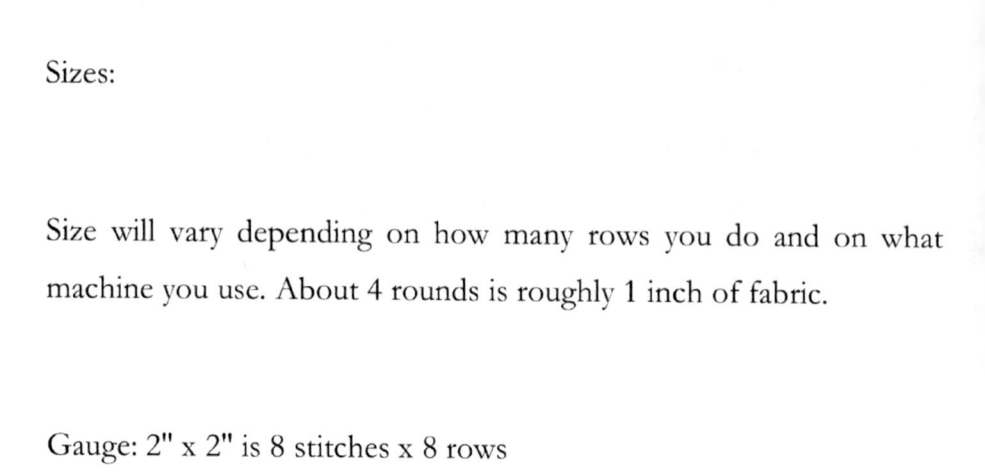

Sizes:

Size will vary depending on how many rows you do and on what machine you use. About 4 rounds is roughly 1 inch of fabric.

Gauge: 2" x 2" is 8 stitches x 8 rows

Start with waste yarn and cast on and crank out 10 rounds or so.

Switch to Yarn for the lining and crank out 45 rounds

Loosely tie on main color yarn and crank out 65 rounds for a total of 110 Rounds.

Cast off by using one of the circular knitting needles, transferring all stitches onto the circular needle. You can also use a darning needle but will need to use a different method for binding off and sewing the bottom of the bag.

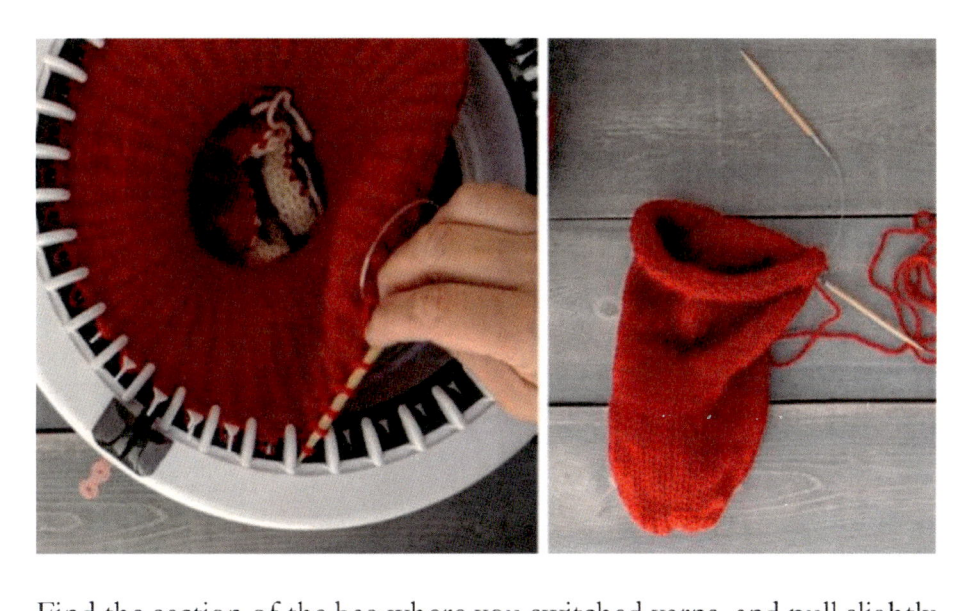

Find the section of the bag where you switched yarns, and pull slightly to straighten up the seam. Tie and trim yarn, leave about an inch on each side of the knot.

Grab your other circular knitting needle and pick up all the stitches from the lining at the bottom of the knit tube. Once all stitches from the bottom have been transferred onto the 2nd circular needle pull off waste yarn.

Circular Knitting Machine Patterns

Grab the bottom of the tube and pull it up to meet the top of the tube, bind off.

Follow the line across the bottom of the bag and stitch under the seam to close bottom of bag.

Circular Knitting Machine Patterns

Add a ribbon to make the bag a drawstring. Use the line from where the lining meets the main color of the bag as a guide.

Circular Knitting Machine Patterns

You can adjust the size of the liner to make more or less of a ruffle at the top, just add more rows of liner if you want less knitted fabric at the top of your bag. Still knit to the 110 rounds if you want a bag this size.

Circular Knitting Machine Patterns

Simple 4-Minute Bow

The number of rows you make will determine the bulkiness or fullness of the bow.

After you crank 25 rows, cut your yarn leaving about a 12-15 inch tail.

Circular Knitting Machine Patterns

Then, thread your tail onto a plastic tapestry needle. Start slowing cranking your yarn machine and picking off the stitches one at a time and pulling your tail through.

After you pick up the last stitch, pull your tail to clinch all the stitches together.

Remove your needle and pull the other sides tail to clinch it shut.

Now we have the main body of our bow made and it's time to squish it into bow shape.

You could also attach these bows to an alligator clip.

Start by making sure your clinch is tight on both ends and that all your stitches are adjusted and have fallen into place.

Circular Knitting Machine Patterns

Begin to scrunch your bow shape, starting in the middle.

Your two cinched ends will be on the top and bottom middle of your bow.

Carefully begin wrapping one of your tails around the center of the bow to hold it into place.

Adjust your bow as you go.

After you have it wrapped a few times, grab the other tail and continue wrapping in the opposite direction.

After a few wraps, give your bow some adjusting and get ready to attach it to your headband or clip.

Lay the bow face down, grab your headband, and continue wrapping your tail around the center this time also going around the headband or clip while the clip is open.

Make a few passes with your tapestry needle hiding your tails between the center wrapping.

After you get your tails sewn in you can cut your yarn, make any final adjustments – then volia!

You have a cute and chunky little bow!